Children of Terror

Children of Terror

✦

*Inge Auerbacher and
Bożenna Urbanowicz Gilbride*

iUniverse, Inc.
New York Bloomington

iUniverse books may be ordered through booksellers or by contacting:

iUniverse
1663 Liberty Drive
Bloomington, IN 47403
www.iuniverse.com
1-800-Authors (1-800-288-4677)

Because of the dynamic nature of the Internet, any Web addresses or links contained in this book may have changed since publication and may no longer be valid. The views expressed in this work are solely those of the author and do not necessarily reflect the views of the publisher, and the publisher hereby disclaims any responsibility for them.

ISBN: 978-1-4401-7809-2 (sc)
ISBN: 978-1-4401-7953-2 (ebook)

Printed in the United States of America

iUniverse rev. date: 11/16/2009

Dedication

*We dedicate this book with our love to
all the children of the world.
Our wish is that they grow up in peace,
without hunger and without prejudice.*

Acknowledgments

JOINT THANKS

We both want to thank our editor, Felicia Friedland Weinberg, who was our pilot and made our manuscript fly and soar above the clouds. Our gratitude goes to Ed Weinberg for his excellent fine-tuning of our work, expert attention to detail and technological help. We are indebted to Professor Richard C. Lukas for granting us permission to use segments from his book, *Forgotten Survivors — Polish Christians Remember The Nazi Occupation*, published by the University Press of Kansas, 2004. Appreciation goes to Lauren Simeone Berman for bringing our pictures to life, and to Professor Shawn Kildea and Gina Grosso, for their encouragement and friendship.

THANKS FROM BOŻENNA

I give special thanks to my husband Dick for taking over the household chores, which allowed me to write this book. He claims to be the only man in town with dishpan hands. Thank you to Stephen Mannino for the illustrations; Liz Macchio for her encouragement; Kathryn Burton of K. Burton/Kitty Kat Graphics for the magnificent photos; Blaine Phelps for teaching me what I needed to know about how to write this book on my computer; and Karolina Matiunin of Lublin, Poland, for the map illustration. I am grateful for the kind words of Bill Donohue of Catholic League for Religious and Civil Rights, and Ambassador

Aldona Wos. Lastly, I want to thank God for our survival and the good health to finish this book.

I dedicate my story to my children, Richard T., Timothy, Stephen and Christine; and to my grandsons, Gregory, Trevor and Richard J.

THANKS FROM INGE

I am grateful to my wonderful friend and soul sister, Bożenna, for co-writing this book with me. I want to also include Bożenna's loving husband Dick, who showed much patience for both of us during the stressful time writing our stories. I am most grateful to my dear friend Aaron Morgan, graphic artist, for the generous contribution of his great artistic talent to our project. Many thanks go to Rabbi Dr. Hirsch Joseph Simckes, of the St John's University Department of Theology, for being my friend, and for always being there for me. Deep gratitude goes to David G. Marwell, Ph.D, Director of the Museum of Jewish Heritage — A Living Memorial to the Holocaust, for sharing his kindness and wisdom. I am grateful to my dear friend Seymour L. Goldstein for being the wind beneath my wings, forever giving me inspiration, guidance, and the encouragement to go on and never give up. I am immensely grateful to my parents for their eternal love, and to God for keeping me safe in his divine embrace.

Contents

ABOUT THE AUTHORS

Prologue

During the Holocaust of World War II, eleven million innocent people were killed. Much has been written about the six million Jews, and very little about the five million "others." Among them were millions of Christian Poles.

Bożenna, a practicing Roman Catholic from Poland, and Inge, an observant Jew from Germany, were born in 1934, a few months apart from each other. They met many years later in the United States when they both participated in a high school seminar on the Holocaust. They felt a similarity in their experiences, and have been friends ever since.

Inge was recently a houseguest at Bożenna's home on Long Island, New York. They went for a walk. Two shadows formed on the ground in the dimming sunlight. Inge, being taller than Bożenna, stepped back slightly in order to equalize the height of the shadows. As the shadows became twins, Bożenna said, "Can you tell the difference?"

The idea was born that they write a book together, comparing their lives and experiences as children growing up in a time of terror.

Bożenna's
Story

Home Sweet Home

I was born on October 12, 1934 to Wiktor and Janina Urbanowicz, in the small village of Leonowka, located in the far eastern province of Wolyn in Poland. Its population of 300 consisted primarily of Ukrainian Christians and, like my family, Polish Roman Catholics. The meld also included a small group of Polish and Ukrainian Jews.

No one talked about his or her ethnic roots; religion was not an issue. Whenever they met on their way to the market or church, people just talked about their crops and how they were doing.

I could name all the families in the village, but families didn't socialize with each other because they worked such long hours and had no extra energy to visit. However, everyone learned from everyone else. To this day I still count some beautiful Jewish recipes as part of my cooking repertoire, along with my Polish, American and Irish dishes.

I was the oldest of four children and was delivered, like almost everyone else, by the town's midwife. My parents were dark-haired and of medium height. I was followed two years later by my brother, Czeslaw, and in another two years by my sister, Irena. Baby Krystyna was born one year later. Though my mother had four children within six years, she also worked hard in the fields, and as the oldest I was responsible for watching my siblings, even from a very young age.

My mother christened me Bożenna, which means "of God." My second name is Boguslawa, meaning "praise be to God." It is still a puzzle to me what my mother expected of her first-born child, but I helped as much as I could. I tried very hard to live up to my name.

We lived in a typical Polish one-story farmhouse, painted gray and white. The house stood back from the street. Walking down a short path, one would enter a tiny *ganek* (porch), which was followed by a large living room with cheerful green plants lining the many windows. The *ganek* had a bench on either side, but we didn't have much time to sit there. A long bedroom ran the length of the house.

All of us slept in the bedroom. My bed was right under the window, and not too far outside was the chicken coop. The rooster woke me up early every morning with his "cock-a-doodle-do," which was a great annoyance to me.

Near the fireplace, there were two more beds where my siblings slept. The girls slept in one bed, my brother in the other. My parent's place was at the far end of the long room. There was also a kitchen and dining room area, which had a trap door opening into the root cellar, a cool area where perishable food was stored.

Every room had a crucifix on the wall. My brother, sisters and I said our prayers both in the morning and at night, with our mother listening attentively. We said the "Our Father," along with a prayer to the Guardian Angel. Since we were not close with our neighbors due to everyone's hard work schedule and style of life, the unity of our family, which included our prayer time, was very important to us.

To the right of the house there was an orchard with apple and cherry trees. If we had an overabundance of cherries, my mother would sell what she couldn't can, either for money or more likely for barter. We had plenty of land for growing crops, and enough land for the cows and horses to graze on. In the nut orchard we had a root cellar, where we stored meat, vegetables and fruit for the winter months. We were basically self-sufficient; what we didn't have we bartered for, as did many of our neighbors.

Across the road but also part of our property there was a shed, where my father would eventually hide people fleeing from the Nazis. My father, who at the age of 30 was the last son to be married, inherited the land from his parents. It consisted of approximately 50 acres. He also owned a portion of the surrounding forest, which provided firewood and wood for repairs of the house, barns and stables.

Stables and barns surrounded our compound. We owned cows, horses, pigs, sheep and chickens. When I was old enough, one of my chores was to take the cows out to pasture each morning. I hated the job because I had to get up very early, rain or shine, while my siblings were allowed to sleep. They were still too young to help.

It was also my chore to round up the cows after their day of grazing. The cows were not always eager to go home and they made my job very difficult. When I finally reached the gate, my father would be there to open it, and I would herd the cows into the compound. One of my rewards was getting warm milk after my mother milked a cow. With the hearty liquid's white foam floating on top, I sipped my treat slowly, relishing the warm nectar as it filled my mouth.

At harvest time my father hired people to help with the gathering of wheat, vegetables, or whatever was growing at the time. My mother also worked in the fields. A Ukrainian girl was hired to take care of us during my mother's absence. We all loved her and called her *nianka* (nanny). Nianka was lots of fun, and she played many games with us, her dark long braids swinging gaily as she moved.

We had no extra money; therefore we had no toys and no car. However, we all had many responsibilities and chores to take care of. On the rare occasion that we had a moment to play, I had the best kind of dolls to play with — live ones, my brother and sisters. We were poor but we didn't know it, since we always had food for our table. Because all our neighbors lived in the same circumstances, there was no comparison of different styles of living or different socioeconomic levels.

I had no human friends other than my siblings, since work on the farm left little time to socialize with other children. But I had a dog with many puppies. And my father bought a horse, which we named Myszka, or Mousie.

Father tried to teach me to ride Myszka without a saddle. When Myszka bent down to graze the grass, I would slide down her neck and land on the ground. My father would laugh with gusto, pick me up and put me back on the horse. But I would soon slide off again. I was disappointed that I could not ride as well as my father.

One way to feed our family was to crush wheat and make flour. This was done by our two horses, one of them Myszka, walking in a circle, around and around a stone mill. My father taught me how to keep the horses walking in circles.

One day as I was walking the horses, I suddenly fell for no apparent reason. I did not realize that I was now in the way of the plodding horses and thus in great danger. My mother, who was watching, screamed, "Bożenna! Bożenna!" but even then I did not understand that the horses were about to trample me.

Fortunately Myszka recognized me and stepped gently over my fallen form. Father told this story many times, since it was unusual for a horse to recognize that a child was in mortal danger and to react accordingly and so quickly. I loved Myszka with all my heart.

In the winter we rode on a large sleigh to church in the neighboring town of Tuczyn, which was 15 minutes away by sleigh, one hour when we walked. We dressed warmly to ward off the biting winds of the cold Polish winter, huddling together under warm dark blankets. I can still hear the bells that were fastened around the two horses' necks, clanging loudly in the silent morning.

During the summer we walked to church carrying our sandals in our hands. Just before arriving at the church, we would visit the Friedmans, a Jewish family who lived a few doors from the church. Before entering their house, I would brush the sand off my feet and put on my sandals. We thought nothing of walking barefoot for the hour-long walk. This was just something that we always did. It never occurred to me that it was to save the cost of shoe repair or replacement.

We sat together with the Friedmans for a while, and then continued our walk to church. The inside of the church had a blue choir loft, and I thought the choir was magnificent. I would often turn around in my seat to look at the choir in the back, and my mother would gently turn me around to face the altar.

My father knew Mr. Friedman from the village open market where he sold or bartered potatoes, other vegetables and flour. One time Mr. Friedman, in payment for some goods, had nothing to give my father except a pair of white high-boot galoshes. They were meant for me, but I remember thinking, "What will I ever do with white galoshes?" After all, I was a farm girl. I had to be in the barn, and I was surrounded by mud. I had no use for such fine things.

I placed the white galoshes on a shelf like a trophy, and looked at them often, hoping that one day I would have a chance to wear them. But that day never came.

In our garden to the left of our house there were fragrant lilac bushes and a beautiful acacia tree. Daffodils found a home right under the kitchen window. In our orchard, in addition to our cherry and apple trees, we grew blueberry bushes. There was always a lot of shade to hide from the blazing sun, whenever I had time. My only problem, as I mentioned before, was that I had very little time to do anything after my chores were finished.

There were no big shops in our little village of Leonowka. We had to go to the nearby city of Tuczyn to do any extra marketing. There was only one candy store in Leonowka, where we bought sweets at Christmas and Easter time. Tuczyn, however, had a lot of stores and lots of goodies, which we stared at somewhat wistfully on the rare times that we had a few minutes to enjoy the bigger town.

During Christmas a tree was set up in the kitchen/dining room area. It stood on top of a long bench in the corner of the room. I never understood why there was always a bucket of water nearby, but the danger of the tree catching fire was always a possibility. We clipped candles on the branches of the tree and lit them only after nightfall. We sang carols together and then carefully blew the candles out, saving the remains for the next day.

In Polish, Christmas Eve is called *Wigilia* (the vigil), and is celebrated in a very special way. The dinner table is set with straw underneath a white tablecloth, reminding us of the stable where Jesus was born. The family shares the blessed wafer, called the *oplatek*, received earlier from the church. When the first star appears in the sky, a meatless dinner begins.

In our house, Christmas was more a religious holiday than a day of gift giving. We were too little to go to midnight Mass, but we all went to services on Christmas Day itself. It was a happy day, a day of rest from work, with only the necessities being done. We were happy to play together quietly and made no demands on our parents.

Christmas morning was very exciting. Although we did not exchange gifts, sometimes we received a new coat and warm mittens with a matching scarf, knitted by our mother. We never saw her knitting them, so the precious gifts were a big surprise.

We then went to church in our sleigh. After church services, relatives came to visit. We had a large family of aunts, uncles, many cousins, and grandparents.

During the long winter, we sometimes had a dance at our house. One of my uncles played the violin, another an accordion, a third the clarinet. One of my aunts sang and played the guitar. We had to move all the furniture away from the middle of the floor, lining everything up against the wall to make room for the dancers.

There was never any liquor. We drank homemade fruit juice made from plums, a rare treat. My brother, sisters and I watched excitedly as the women twirled around, skirts billowing until the music stopped. We hoped that one day we could join them as they danced the day away.

Easter was also a very important holiday for us. It meant the blessing of a modest basket of food brought to church by a member of the family or by a neighbor the day before Easter. On Easter Sunday morning we hitched two horses to our buggy and went clip-clopping to our church in Tuczyn.

It was a custom not to eat anything until after the service. Our family then shared hard-boiled eggs from the food basket that had been blessed the previous day. After that we continued our breakfast, eating the rest of the blessed food, feeling great joy.

The blessed egg symbolized a new beginning, a new life. Sometimes we received new clothes in honor of the occasion. One year I received a new white dress with a dark blue trim and matching sash. We were always told to keep our clothes clean; we knew that it would be a long time before we received new clothes again.

I remember a picture that was taken of my brother, my sister Irena and me. My mother wanted me to wear the white dress I had gotten for Easter, but the blue sash was missing. Mother was in a panic looking for the sash, which she finally found. We posed, smiling with relief, as the photographer finally took the picture. Everyone used this particular photographer for special occasions, which were rare and far between.

Our house in Leonowka

Father and his sisters
Coming home from church in Tuczyn, about 1937-1938

From left: Czeslaw, Bożenna and Irena
Leonowka, Easter, about 1940

The Red Storm

Danger was in the air. Germany's Nazi hordes invaded Poland on September 1, 1939, occupying two-thirds of western Poland. The Soviet Union followed, entering eastern Poland on September 17, 1939. I was then almost five years old. Our lives changed drastically when Leonowka came under Soviet occupation. We suddenly were in the midst of the "Red Storm."

My father placed little red flags along the front of our white picket fence to show our solidarity with the Russian soldiers marching through our village. As soon as the soldiers were out of sight, I was told to remove the flags. This procedure was repeated many times.

The new Communist regime instituted collective farms, which meant that we had to give up part of our farm and animal products to the Russians. It was forbidden to slaughter a pig or cow without permission. Even when we got permission, most of the meat had to be turned over to the new authorities.

My father devised a plan to outsmart the regime. He invited two or three neighbors to kill a pig at night, dividing the meat among them. By using this plan, none of the neighbors was willing to turn in the other. Done in complete secrecy, turns were taken among the neighbors to supply the pig for slaughter.

Eventually, father was caught and sent to jail for a few days. We children were told nothing about the reason for his absence. We just knew that he wasn't at home, that he was probably visiting a relative. During the Communist regime, Father, who had beehives in our orchard, was ordered to give a portion of our honey to the Communists. The Communists demanded a percentage of everything that was grown or raised on our farm. A man once came to our house with a net over his face to protect him from bee stings. He collected a large amount of the honey, leaving the small remainder for us.

The school we attended was near our house, and I was able to walk there. At Christmas time our teacher told us that the Russians would be coming to inspect our school.

The inspectors asked, "Who gives you candy?" We answered loudly as our teacher taught us, "Papa Stalin gives us candy." The Russians wanted us to believe that Stalin, the brutal Soviet dictator, gave us the candy, not Santa Claus. Under Soviet control, all religions were officially banned. After we chanted "Papa Stalin," we were given lemon drops called *landrynki* for giving the right answer. We all loved the sweet treat.

In the winter of 1940-1941, my aunt and uncle, who was an officer in the Polish Army, along with their three children, were ordered to be deported to Siberia. But a neighbor had warned them of the plans, and our relatives came to us in the middle of the night in an attempt to escape their fate. The Communists found them at our house and deported the whole family to the *gulags*, the Russian prison camps in Siberia. My father was arrested for helping them, and again spent some time in jail.

Inferno

Just before attacking Poland, Hitler told his army: "Kill without pity or mercy all men, women and children of the Polish race and language. Only in such a way will we win the vital space that we need. My pact with Poland was only meant to stall for time . . . Be hard . . . Be without mercy. The citizens of Western Europe must quiver in horror."

In 1941, Germany invaded the Soviet-occupied portion of Poland, and then the Soviet Union proper, which meant that all of Poland was now under Nazi rule. My town, Leonowka, was now under the Nazi occupation. Nazi policy was to eliminate all Polish culture and to eradicate its people through mass executions and by sending us to concentration camps. Not only were Polish Christians murdered and sent to camps, but the Jewish minority was especially targeted for extermination. Hitler had a special hatred against the Slavic people and the Jews.

When the Nazis entered Poland, I no longer attended school. All schooling was forbidden. On May 15, 1940, Heinrich Himmler, the Chief of the SS, decreed that Polish children were to be educated only so far as to be able to sign their own name, to be obedient to the Germans, to read simple instructions, and not to be able to count further than 500.

Polish priests were rounded up and sent to Dachau concentration camp. All Polish intellectuals, doctors, lawyers, teachers and civic leaders were arrested and sent to concentration camps. A concentration camp for Polish youth was established in Lodz, in the vicinity of Dzierzania. Polish children were abducted off the streets and sent to Germany for adoption and "Germanization." We knew what was waiting for us. Our fates were in the hands of the occupying Nazis. We had no government of our own and no one to protect us.

My parents hid people we didn't know in our shed near the river. I was told to bring them food when there was no one around to see me. Mother warned that if I was stopped on the road I should speak to no one and return home immediately.

I never knew if these people were men, women or children. All I saw were outstretched hands grabbing the food, and then the partially open door closing quickly. It wasn't until after the war that the secret came out, that the hands belonged to Jews. By overhearing my father telling some close relatives, "You should have seen what they did to our Jews," I finally discovered that my parents had been helping them.

One time when my father was caught helping the Jews, he was sent to jail and interrogated. He revealed nothing, and came home after a few days. In Poland, helping Jews was punishable by death. Many Poles perished for doing what my father did.

Once again, we children were told nothing about why he was away. I don't know to this day how my father, who was arrested so many times, was so lucky to be allowed out of prison again and again. It was a miracle how he managed to walk away each time unscathed.

Our lives changed forever in August of 1943, shortly before I was nine years old. The Ukrainian People's Army or UPA (*Ukraynska Povstanska Armia*), a nationalist partisan organization which collaborated with the Nazis, independently decided to kill all the Christian and Jewish Poles in Wolyn.

At nine years of age, I had no idea what the UPA was. But I realized in a very short time that they were a group to be feared. That summer our neighbors and we had to sleep in the fields to avoid being killed by the UPA. One of the adults would climb a tall tree to act as the lookout and guard. The next night a different adult had the responsibility. Weeks later, my father said that he had had enough of sleeping in the field. He said, "We will sleep in our beds tonight." But about 11 o'clock that evening, after we had returned home, a neighbor knocked on my window, which had been left open in the warm August night.

"Wiktor, Wiktor, this is the night." My parents knew what this meant: Leonowka was now under siege by the UPA. My mother awakened us quietly. I was told to get some sweaters off the hooks, since it could get chilly at night. But I saw my parents and my siblings rushing out the door, and became fearful of being left behind. Forgetting about the sweaters, I ran after my parents and siblings. I had no idea that I would never see my home again.

When we reached the main road, I thought that my father was planning to cross the bridge and head for Tuczyn. But we saw that Leonowka was burning on the left side where the school and bridge was. Quickly we turned to the right instead, in the direction of Grandma's house.

Going this way became impossible as well, since everything was in flames on the right side also. The UPA was burning our village from both ends. We were trapped in the middle.

I remember seeing shadows of people running across the road. I heard a great deal of screaming. At first I thought that it was the animals that were screaming. Then I realized that people were screaming as well. You could not distinguish one sound from the other; it was pure chaos, horror and fear.

We ran into the wheat fields for protection, because at that time of the year the wheat was tall. My mother carried my baby sister, Krystyna. I was told to hold the hands of my brother Czeslaw and my sister Irena, and to follow quickly.

My mother's steps were longer and faster than mine, and she was rapidly getting ahead of us. The wheat tangled around my feet, and when I stumbled in the vines, my siblings fell along with me. By the time we got up, Mother was even further away. I was terrified of losing her, but I didn't dare to cry out.

Suddenly I heard the crackling of wheat behind me. Someone was running after me! I was too scared to look back or, once again, to call out to my mother, in case someone might hear me. My mother, looking back to make sure that we were still behind her, saw a man running after us in the moonlight. She gasped. Fear was written all over her face.

"Janka," the man whispered, as he grabbed my brother and sister from me and ran to my mother. It was my father. He had remained behind to free the animals from the barns and stables. We still had hopes of returning to our house after the terror of the night ended.

Some of our neighbors hid with us in the wheat fields. All night we continued to hear the crackling sound of burning homes, and the anguished cries of people screaming. We cowered together, fearing the worst.

Grandma's house was behind us, separated from us by the forest. Fearful thoughts crossed my mind. "If the trees catch fire," I thought, "the wheat fields will surely burn as well. We will be exposed, and they will kill us."

My baby sister started to cry. We held our breaths, fearing that the enemy would hear her. Quickly my mother cuddled Krystyna, rocking her to sleep. We huddled together, a chill and fear in the air. No one other than my little sister dared to fall asleep. We feared to even whisper. And we waited.

In the morning it was quiet and eerie. Silently we crossed the shallow river. As we reached an open field, we heard shots. We fell to the ground as one, and began to crawl to the nearby forest. The UPA was still hunting the people of Leonowka, shouting to each other as if they were participating in a foxhunt.

In our rush to leave home, we had never changed clothes, and were still in our nightshirts. One of my aunts and her family lived in the forest. We approached their house cautiously, hoping that they had survived the massacre. No one was at home and my parents assumed the worst — that they had run away and would never be seen again, or that they had been killed.

In order to get to the main road, we had to pass a pond near the house. As we walked past it, three figures stood up. We thought that we had been caught and would be killed by the UPA, but to our surprise it was my aunt, uncle and their teenage son. They had spent the night hiding in the pond. We were so relieved to find them alive.

Another aunt and her family lived on the main road to Tuczyn. We soon came to their house. The door was wide open and it seemed deserted, except for the geese and chickens running freely throughout the rooms. My mother quickly pulled some clothing out of a drawer and dressed us warmly. She found some bread and cut it into slices, patting them with butter and sprinkled sugar. This was such an unusual treat in the midst of the horror surrounding us. While it was wonderful, it was also almost surreal, a drop of normalcy in an ocean of fear.

Had we known that we would never see my aunt and her family again and never find out what happened to them, the bread would not have tasted nearly as sweet.

1943: Deportation to Germany

When we arrived on the streets of Tuczyn, we found throngs of people streaming in from all directions. This was the first time that I saw German soldiers. They were pushing and shoving us, herding us toward the unknown. Mothers held babies in their arms. Some pushed baby carriages, others carried bundles. We ourselves had little to carry, since we had lost almost everything in the fire.

It was dark when we arrived at the railway station in the city of Rowne. The German soldiers told us that we could sleep at the warehouse near the railroad station. Some people accepted their offer, but my father did not want to be trapped inside a building.

The Germans told us, "The UPA will come to finish you off tonight. But we will give you guns to shoot back."

Years later we learned that this was a ploy by the Germans, who wanted the Poles and the UPA to kill each other, thus saving the Germans the trouble and energy of killing us themselves.

It was late summer and still warm. There was an embankment near the railroad station, and we slept on the ground, blanketed by the sky. There was a lot of shooting by the UPA that night. Young Polish men who had been given guns shot back at the UPA all through the night. I remember bullets whizzing over my head. My father kept pushing me down. "Bożenna, keep your head down." Fortunately, no one in my family was hit.

The Germans collected the guns in the morning, and made us an offer that was hard to refuse: "You can stay in Poland and be finished off by the UPA, or we will take you to Germany," they told us. "It will be good in Germany. You will be fed, you will be clothed, adults will have work and children will go to school," they assured us.

Hardly waiting for an answer, we were quickly led toward the waiting cattle cars. I learned my first German word as the soldiers yelled, "*Schnell, Schnell,*" meaning "be quick."

In the confusion my father was separated from us. Mother poked her head out of the wagon, screaming, "Wiktor, Wiktor, where are you?"

My father, still on the railroad platform, heard my mother's voice and pushed through the crowd. People helped him up into our wagon. Our family was together once again.

The cattle car was packed with many people. I had never been on a train before, and had no idea what a train should be like. The car had no windows, only a slit on top, which let in a little air. There was an awful smell because of the poor sanitary conditions. A young Polish mother standing next to me holding an infant in her arms begged for some space to nurse her baby. But there was little space to be had.

We traveled for about three days. The doors were never opened, although the train stopped often. We were never given an explanation for the pauses. We had very little food with us, and no new provisions were distributed. Some older people sat crowded together on the floor, others remained standing huddled together in groups, trying all the while to squeeze in and find some space to sit on the floor.

Finally the doors of the cattle cars were opened. We had arrived in Germany. Once again the command, "*Schnell, Schnell,*" was screamed, and hundreds of people spilled out of the wagons onto the train platform, trying to get their cramped and swollen legs to obey the orders. We were quickly divided into groups of about thirty people each. Our group was selected to go to Freiberg. Thankfully our family was still together.

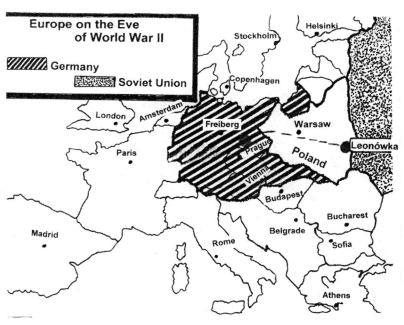

Deportation to Germany

Freiberg, Germany

We arrived in Freiberg in early September, 1943, and were housed in an old school building. There were no beds, so we had to sleep on the floor. Using our rolled-up clothes as pillows, we closed our eyes, waiting with apprehension for the next day to arrive.

My parents were forced to work at a tannery, where they made leather goods for the German war effort. Many of the children worked outside, preparing the fields for the next planting. Since both my parents worked in the factory, it became my responsibility to take care of my three younger siblings.

We had no warm clothing, and I became very sick during the winter. No one knew what was the matter with me. My mother told her German foreman at the tannery about my worsening condition, that I was having trouble walking, and that I lay on the floor all day.

One day while my parents were at work in the tannery, the German foreman came to see me. He motioned with his finger to follow him. I already knew to obey the Germans, so even in my weakened condition I struggled to follow him down the cold, slippery iron flight of stairs. I was trembling with illness, and afraid that I might slip through the open spaces between each step.

A small black car was waiting for us. I was put in the back seat. I wondered if my parents knew what was happening to me. I tried to memorize landmarks in case I decided to run away and return to my family. But I was too ill to remember anything.

I saw a big city, and thought that since I was so sick, the man was taking me to a hospital. After that everything became a blur. The man soon stopped at a small wooden barracks, and said, "This is for people like you." I had no idea what he meant by the remark, but I followed instructions and weakly entered the building.

The foreman placed me in the care of two German women. I was told to undress and put on a white nightshirt. Since my hair was infested with lice, the women shaved my head. One "nurse" placed me in a small room containing six empty beds. It had one little window. From my bed I looked out the window often, hoping to see people or cars, but all I saw were mountains with white peaks. Too sick to move, I stayed in bed wondering who would look after my brother and sisters when my parents went to work.

In childish protest at being separated from my family, I deliberately wet my bed. I refused to open my eyes when the women angrily changed my sheets, bouncing me from one bed to another. I was not punished for my actions. Perhaps the women felt a little pity for me, lying there so sick and so alone.

As I got a little better, I could hear voices of children elsewhere in the barracks, but no one was ever permitted to share my room. I never learned how old the other children were, or what illnesses they suffered from.

In one of my dreams, I imagined my mother sitting next to my bed, lovingly stroking my hand. As she touched me gently, I tried not to cry. Desperately trying to hold onto her dreamlike presence, I kept my eyes closed so that the dream would not fade away. I needed to hold onto the image of her presence, in case that was all that it was.

Years later I learned that my mother really had come to see me. She wanted to be sure I was still alive.

The Germans informed my parents that I had dysentery and tuberculosis, a contagious disease that would require isolation for a long time. They were afraid that I would infect them and the forced laborers in the camp, which is why they removed me.

They were of course not concerned with us as human individuals, they merely didn't want to take the chance of losing any other manpower to illness.

A different German man came to pick me up after about three months. He was on a bicycle and I had to sit on the handlebars as we rode along, holding on for dear life. There was melting snow on the ground, and the mud splashed on my legs. During our ride, I prayed that I was being returned to my family. My prayers were answered, but the German refused my mother's plea to allow me to rest for an extra day before returning to work.

When I awoke the next morning, I couldn't find my shoes. Someone had stolen them during the night. I had to wrap my feet in rags as I had seen other children do. I returned to work clearing the fields for next season's planting, taking my brother and younger sister along. It was very cold, and we had no gloves or warm clothing. Our hands and feet were ice cold. We shivered the whole time.

My baby sister was cared for by the few mothers who were excused from outside work and assigned to take care of other babies, as well as their own.

Soon after, we were ordered to pack our few belongings. We were being relocated to another place. Old trucks and horse-drawn wagons arrived, and we were told to ride in one of the trucks. Once again we headed into the unknown.

1944: Chemnitz Labor Camp

As we traveled through a city whose name I do not remember, we were suddenly stopped to make way for a parade. My father and I stepped down from the truck to join the crowd watching the parade. My father pointed with excitement. "Bożenna, Bożenna, look! That is Adolf Hitler in the parade." He lifted me onto his shoulders to get a better view.

I hardly knew who Hitler was — I knew that he was important, and that people were paying great attention to him — but I didn't know why. I was more interested in the two-seater motorcycle he was riding in. I had never seen such a wonderful machine before.

Soon we were on the road again, eventually arriving at a labor camp in eastern Germany. The Chemnitz Labor Camp was very different from Freiberg. The Germans had enclosed the camp with a high fence topped with barbed wire. There were wooden barracks housing people of different nationalities. Poles, Ukrainians and Gypsies milled together regardless of background.

After our arrival in Chemnitz, the Germans told us that the children would receive milk. They actually followed through on this promise and distributed cups to us. I got in line for my share, being careful not to spill a drop of the precious liquid. When I looked into my cup to see how much I had received, I noticed that only the bottom of the container was covered with milk.

The milk distribution was not repeated again. We were given some bread, which tasted funny, not like the bread we ate in

Poland. I ate it because I was always hungry and knew that it would be a long time before I got bread again.

The camp was located between the Chemnitz railroad station and a munitions factory, where the prisoners were forced to work. My father had the day shift, loading torpedoes onto trucks that took the weapons to railroad cars waiting nearby. Mother worked the night shift at the same factory, so we hardly had any time together as a family.

We were forbidden to look from the window of the barracks at the railroad station. The German guards threatened to shoot us if we did. A curious child, I defied the threats, and the sign "Chemnitz" on the railroad station is embedded in my brain to this day.

The reason for these orders was that the Germans feared some of the prisoners might be spies, able to time the train schedules and make note of which direction ammunition carriers were headed. As it was, air raid sirens wailed day and night as the Allies tried to bomb the railroad station, the tracks and the munitions factory. All of this made us nervous and scared, as there was absolutely no place for us to escape to in the event that a bomb successfully hit its mark.

I remember the day a picture was taken by a new Polish arrival at the camp. The Germans failed to find her camera and she quickly took a picture of a group of us standing in front of our barracks. I was terrified because I knew that it was not allowed.

Our barracks housed around twenty people, all of us from Poland. We slept on double-deck bunk beds with mattresses made of straw. I was on the upper level. There was no other furniture, so we sat on our beds, and they became the totality of our home. Sometimes at night I thought of our house in Leonowka, and wondered if our dog and puppies had survived the fire.

There was no toilet in our barracks. We had to use the latrine, the public toilet, near the barracks. I was terrified to go there by myself, never certain of whom I would meet, or what they might want from me. The camp rule was that no prisoner was ever allowed to be outside the camp unless under guard.

But there were times at night, with sirens wailing, when the Allies would attempt to bomb the tracks or the ammunition factory. Our barracks were right next to the track and so we were right in the path of their attempts. My father had loosened some slats in the fence near our barracks, which only my family knew about. If another family or individual found out about this, they might have snitched on us, hoping for more scraps of food for themselves. During those bombing raids, we scurried to our loosened slats, trying not to be seen by the Germans who lived close to the camp. We hurried back to our barracks as soon as the bombing stopped, relieved that once again we had not been caught.

Children were not forced to work. I made no friends in the camp since I trusted no one. My only friends were my siblings. We had no toys. I do not remember any act of kindness shown to us by the guards.

We did not cook our meals in the barracks, although there was a wood-burning stove in the far corner from where our family slept. There was a community kitchen operated by the Germans, where some prisoners worked. I recall big pots of turnip soup being brought to us. Small portions of the murky liquid were ladled out into bowls and we ate with old bent spoons. We ate either in the barracks or outside, if the weather was good and we were not being bombed. The other prisoners ate at the munitions factory during their work schedules.

After one of the bombing raids, a portion of the fence was knocked down. Curious, I carefully moved toward the opening to see what was on the other side.

To my surprise I saw a garbage dump. I thought, where there is garbage there must be food. I got on all fours and quietly crawled to the dumpsite. I did not want anyone to see me; my actions could result in punishment or death.

I wore a dress, so my bare knees were in the garbage. I found apple peels, which I ate fast and furiously. I searched for more, but found potato peels instead. Scooping them up, I placed them in my dress, holding the dress out like an apron. My plan was to carry my bounty back to the barracks.

Before I stood, I looked up and saw a beautiful white house on a hill overlooking the dump. It was dusk, and I could see a lit chandelier in a room on the second floor. With tears in my eyes I sadly recognized the contrast of me eating in the garbage dump, while someone on the hill was living with the luxury of a chandelier.

To this day, I cannot get out of my mind the picture of myself as a little girl digging like a dog for scraps of food, while on the hill overlooking me people were living in a magnificent home with a chandelier. Sadly I returned to our barracks and gave the potato peels to a woman who washed and cooked them. I do not remember eating them, and I felt quite guilty for eating all the apple peels and not sharing them with my family.

Another time the camp kitchen was bombed, and I saw broken jars of red jelly on the ground. I decided to eat some of the delicacy. I could hardly remember the taste of jelly, since we had not had this treat since we left Leonowka. Placing some in my hand, I tried to bring the jelly back to the barracks in order to share it. To my disappointment, by the time I reached the barracks, all I had left was an empty, sticky red hand. The jelly had trickled through my fingers.

I recall another bombing raid. Once again the target was supposed to be the factory. We were ordered to leave the camp and the Germans marched us, for some unknown reason, outside the camp. The bomb missed the intended target and left a large crater in the ground, which soon filled with water. My parents, my siblings and I wound up at the edge of the crater. Next to us was a German guard holding a rifle. He told my father that he "couldn't wait until Hitler won the war and all of this would be over." My father did not dare to answer him, in case his words were a trap. Meanwhile, planes dropped leaflets telling Hitler to surrender. "The war is lost. The people will soon be freed."

The only shower I had during all the time I was in Germany remains a very clear recollection. We were taken to the basement of the munitions factory, told to undress and pile each family's belongings together. My parents were very quiet and told us to do as we were instructed.

We stood naked inside the shower stalls and waited. My parents huddled us closely together. I was very embarrassed to see my parents naked. We waited some more. Suddenly, cold water burst out of the showerhead. My parents looked frightened, but said nothing. They just kept holding us tightly.

We were then told to stand in front of huge hot air vents. My parents lined us up without saying a word. We stood and waited. After a few moments we heard, and then felt, warm air rushing in. My parents frightened me when they suddenly gasped, but shortly afterward we were told to get dressed and return to our barracks.

My father never told me why he was so afraid of the showers and the hot air vents. But apparently he had somehow known about the gassing in the other concentration camps.

Even during those horrific times, I never lost my faith in God. Since the German Nazis wanted nothing to do with religion, my mother told me to say my prayers in private while lying down on my bunk bed. At home I would kneel down near my bed. I thought this new way of praying was very disrespectful, and not very Christian. But I was an obedient child and I followed my mother's advice. So did my sisters and brother, who copied what I did.

Chemnitz Labor Camp, 1944
Last row, from left: Mother
Middle row, from left: Czeslaw, Irena and Bożenna (in beret)
Front row, from left: Krystyna

Bożenna in garbage dump at Chemnitz Labor Camp, 1945

1944-1945: Chemnitz — Mother Arrested

During the winter of 1944-1945, the Germans arrested my father at the factory and interrogated him all night. They beat him terribly for allegedly writing a personal letter that criticized the Germans for their bad treatment of slave laborers, lack of food and medical attention for the children.

The following morning, after my father had been beaten and was totally exhausted, he was shown the letter and asked whose signature was at the bottom. He admitted, without thinking, that it was my mother's. The letter was meant to reach my mother's brother in another camp, but had been intercepted by the guards. My father was sent back to work his regular day shift, although he had not slept all night.

In the morning two German policemen came to arrest my mother, dragging her away. She looked back at me with terror in her eyes and whispered, "Bożenna, there are nine marks under the mattress."

I had no idea what I was supposed to do with the money. I stood helplessly, watching my mother disappear outside the campgrounds.

This began my mother's terrible odyssey. Mother never returned to the camp. A foreman at the factory told my father that my mother was sent to the Ravensbrueck concentration camp for women, located in Germany.

After my mother's arrest, my siblings and I remained with our father in the same barracks, and otherwise life at the camp continued as usual. I became the "little mother" to my siblings. We had no one but each other. My father did what he could, but he was away working many hours each day.

I was only ten years old.

When the air raid sirens sounded, other children had mothers to tell them what to do. I felt helpless, and often stood in the middle of the camp crying until my father came home from his shift at the factory.

Children were not forced to work in Chemnitz. Instead, we were required to learn from German women guards whose job was to teach us about Germany, Hitler and the Nazis, and most importantly, about the promising future that awaited everyone after the Germans won the war.

December of 1944 stands out in my mind. Christmas was approaching when the so-called teachers brought us green wool to knit scarves. I liked the color, and looked forward to finishing my scarf and wearing it to keep me warm. But to my disappointment, when the scarves were completed, the German women took them home to their families as Christmas gifts. We had only the recollection of the warm feeling of the wool to keep us warm.

By this time I had lost interest in myself and attended the required lessons dirty and unkempt. I missed my mother and was very sad most of the time. Before our lessons, a female German guard inspected our faces and hands. When she saw mine, she yanked me out of my seat, shouting, "You are never to come here dirty again."

I lost my balance and fell to the ground. The guard kicked me and yelled, "You see what will happen to you if you come here dirty." As I writhed in pain, my sisters and brother watched in fear. After that incident I was even more afraid of everyone and suspicious of everything.

1945: Into the Unknown

In the spring of 1945, the Germans told us that we were being relocated. I did not want to leave, because I worried about how our mother would find us. We had no idea where she was, and I wanted to wait for her return.

One morning several horse-drawn wagons arrived and took us to the outskirts of Chemnitz. The German guards told us to leave the wagons and find the American front. They pointed their guns at us, and told us to never come back. We had no idea where the "front" was. People split into small groups, each with a different idea of where the Allies might be.

Our group consisted of us and one other family. We walked for days, sleeping mostly in the forest, and once in an abandoned railroad car. It was dark inside the railroad car and I was afraid to fall asleep. Thoughts swirled in my head. "What if another train comes and attaches our car to take us to an unknown destination?"

But the morning always arrived without incident, and we continued each day to walk into the unknown. One time my father asked a policeman where the American front was. The policeman became very angry. He would have shot my father, had a German woman not intervened to stop him from pulling the trigger of his gun.

During our journey, we were so hungry that one day we went to a German farmhouse to beg for food. A kind German woman invited us into her house and fed us soup and bread. After eating, we were told to leave from the back door, for fear that someone might see us and harm either the woman or us.

Other than this food, sometimes we would find edible berries and mushrooms as we walked. Eventually we found the Americans, who settled us into an empty building. More and more refugees arrived each day. I had no idea where in Germany we were.

The Americans could not take care of so many homeless people, coming from all directions in the hope of finding shelter. One thought always remained with me: "Where is Mother? Will she know where to find us?"

I was placed in a German school. The German students made fun of me and taunted me with painful slurs.

"You Polish pig, you Polish bandit," was one of their favorite chants. I was dressed shabbily compared to the German children, who appeared well-dressed and clean. The girls even had bows in their hair. I was eleven years old, and how I envied the girls parading in front of me wearing their bows of many colors, resting on top of their neatly combed hair.

We still hadn't gotten any better clothing or good shoes, so it's no wonder that we were made fun of so constantly. However, when the Americans heard how badly we were being treated in school, they decided to send us somewhere else where the living conditions would be better.

Trucks arrived, and our family, minus our mother of course, was driven to an eerie place somewhere in a forest. After we passed through a wide-open gate, the trucks stopped, but no one wanted to get off. When we were asked why we would not move, my father told the Americans that they had taken us to the former Buchenwald concentration camp, which now appeared abandoned.

Understanding our concern and fear of such a place, the Americans immediately returned us to our old living quarters. They had nowhere else to put us.

1945-1946: The Karlsruhe-Forstner DP Camp

Soon after the relocation incident, we were again moved, this time to the Karlsruhe-Forstner DP (displaced persons) camp in southwestern Germany. Here the living conditions were better. The camps were set up by the UNRRA (United Nations Relief and Rehabilitation Administration) to help homeless refugees coming under Allied control.

We were placed in large two- and three-story buildings. I entered the camp school where we had two teachers. A Polish Catholic priest, who had survived a Nazi concentration camp, was in charge of our religious education.

I was eleven years old, and it was high time for me to receive my First Holy Communion and Confirmation. My white dress was made from an old white tablecloth. It was beautiful.

Someone took a picture of my father, my siblings and me standing in the doorway of our block. It says *Blok 4* on each of the doors. I do not remember the name of the church. I think this bit of lost memory was deliberate on my part.

I did not like the German people, their language or their music. Everything German scared me. I chose the name "Mary" for my Confirmation. This was a natural choice for me, since I so desperately wanted a mother. To this day, I have a special devotion to the Blessed Mother.

I was terribly aware that I had no mother, but I did not share my heavy-hearted thoughts with anyone. How I envied those who could find safety in a mother's embrace.

Eventually, in spite of my sadness, I started to make a few friends, and once again I began to trust people.

I tried to cling to everything that was Polish, not to forget all that my mother had taught me to love and cherish. One day I learned that a new girlfriend's Feast or Name Day was coming up. It was a Polish custom to observe the Feast Day instead of a birthday.

I wanted to give my friend flowers as a gift, but where would I get them? I made a plan to go outside the camp to barter a bar of Camay soap, which the UNRRA had given us, in exchange for flowers from someone's garden.

I soon came across a German lady tending her garden, and in my best German asked her if she would trade some flowers for my soap. She agreed, and began picking a big bouquet of mixed flowers for me. My girlfriend was thrilled with the precious gift, and I was equally proud that I had accomplished what I had set out to do.

Being allowed to go anywhere by myself was a new experience for me, and being able to exchange something that I owned for something I wanted was equally a new feeling. This was a truly magical moment in my life.

My First Holy Communion
Father in back
Front, from left: Irena, Krystyna, Bożenna and Czeslaw
Karlsruhe-Forstner DP Camp, 1946

To America

Sometime in 1946, officials of the American wing of UNRRA asked my father what his plans were, now that the war was over. Father answered, "I do not want to return to Poland, since it is now occupied by the Communists. I have had enough of Communism. I can't stay in Germany, because I am afraid of the Germans."

Father told the officials that we had relatives, two brothers and his mother, living in New York City. He had no addresses, but perhaps the organization could locate them. Grandmother had visited her two sons before the war, and luckily was not able to return to Poland after World War II broke out. She was therefore spared the horror that befell Europe.

The officials were successful in finding our relatives, who readily agreed to sponsor us. Almost immediately, visas to America were issued to us. Questions bombarded my mind: "Where is America? Where is my mother? Is she still alive? How will she ever find us?"

In the middle of February 1947, we were on our way to Bremen in a UNRRA car. During our journey we slept in a German woman's home. I slept on a wooden window seat. My sleep was not peaceful, perhaps because I was in a German house, or perhaps due to the excitement of leaving Germany.

We were brought to Bremerhaven, the port of the city of Bremen, and sailed to America on the Ernie Pyle, an American troop transport ship. It was a stormy nine day voyage, and I was seasick the entire trip. But all that mattered was that we were on our way to a new life.

We arrived in the New York City Harbor on February 21, 1947. It was a typical cold winter day, and I was not dressed warmly enough for such freezing weather. I was now twelve years old.

We left the ship, trying to find our land legs. After a long paper process, my uncle was permitted to take us to his home. We drove there in his beautiful blue Chrysler.

I was carsick and my uncle had to stop often to let me out. I could hardly believe it: I was now in a safe place, with lots of family. I even had a grandmother. I wouldn't feel so alone anymore.

I never had a doll, I never jumped rope with friends, and I never wore ribbons in my hair. But beyond this, one immeasurable thought obsessed me every moment during my first years in America: I didn't know if I had a mother anymore. I dreamed of her every night. Had she survived the concentration camp? Was she dead or alive? If she was still alive, she would never think of looking for us in America. She would never find us now.

Aftermath

We settled into an aunt's house in Queens, New York. Our aunt had to take lice out of our hair, which was a terribly humiliating experience. My aunt found me making a rag doll and realized that I had missed that part of growing up. She bought me a paper cutout doll with paper clothes that you can fasten on the doll.

We soon moved to another aunt's house in Brooklyn, where our father enrolled me in a private Polish Catholic school. Although there were no other immigrants in the school, and we had yet to learn English, the nuns and students treated us well.

My father got a job in a textile factory where his brothers worked and eventually bought a house in Brooklyn.

Some time in the winter of 1948-1949, my mother finally located us in America, after experiencing great difficulty in her search. The Communist government would not allow her to leave Poland. We shared letters and pictures frequently.

In high school I studied draping and fashion design as well as sewing. This career earned me a good living until my retirement. American students and teachers took good care of the Poles and Jews who came to America after the war. No one made fun of me anymore.

The years passed. I married an Irish man, Richard V. Gilbride. My younger sister, Irena, married half a year later.

In August 1957, when I was already married and expecting my first baby, my mother arrived in America. She was here for the birth of her first grandchild, the wedding of my brother and my sister Krystyna's entrance into the convent. My four children made my mother a very happy grandmother, but American life in general was difficult for her. She had found her four "children," all grown up, speaking a foreign language she did not understand, living a life whose rules and customs she didn't understand, and she struggled every day to fit in.

I asked my mother many questions about the missing years, and wrote everything down in a journal, but she didn't want to speak about her ordeal in Ravensbrueck and Gross-Rosen concentration camps. She was very embarrassed (it seemed to me) to talk about her ordeal as a prisoner. She died in her sleep before I could ask her to tell me the rest of her story. But I already knew enough. My father refused to speak about the Holocaust. His nightmare screams for "mercy" were heard by all of us, but he still refused to talk about it.

Our children are now grown and married, and I am the proud grandmother of three grandsons. Life in America has been very good.

From left: Irena, Krystyna, Father, Czeslaw and Bożenna
First family photo in Brooklyn, 1947

Sister Boniface in back
Front, from left: Irena, Czeslaw, Krystyna and Bożenna
At the Polish Catholic school in Brooklyn, 1947

Mother in Poland, 1946
Pinned to her dress is her concentration camp prisoner number,
with letter *P* (Polish) below

Nobody Knows

The hunger of everyday . . .
It takes me to the garbage where I may
Find some apple peels today.

I wait for the dusk,
Because I'm afraid if they see me
I will not eat today.

My belly hurts,
But what to do?
Take a risk, take a chance.

It doesn't matter.
I am hungry today and
I must eat today.

Tomorrow is so far away,
Today is what matters.
Today I must eat.

Not a moment to waste,
Hunger is not new to me,
We have known each other
Like a sister and a brother.

So, come what may

I must eat today.

Bożenna Urbanowicz Gilbride

Inge's Story

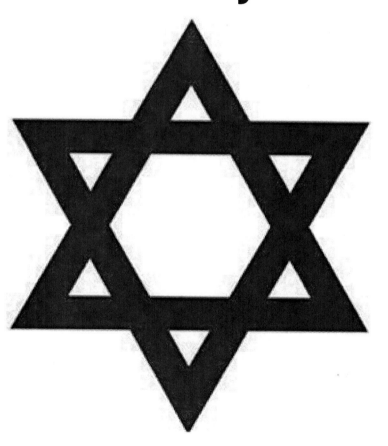

At Home

I was born on December 31, 1934, to Berthold and Regina Auerbacher in Kippenheim, a sleepy village in southwestern Germany at the foot of the Black Forest, close to the borders of France and Switzerland. One has to look carefully on a local map to find it.

The houses lining the streets almost touched each other. A little brook snaked through the street on which our house was located. It was a large house containing seventeen rooms. A few generations of my father's family were born in it.

The population of around 2000 was composed of about 450 Catholic and Protestant families and approximately 60 Jewish families, all living peacefully together. Jews had been living in Kippenheim for at least two hundred years. An only child, I was the last Jewish child born in Kippenheim.

Papa decided that I, like some of his siblings, must be born in the family home rather than in a hospital in the neighboring city. Since Kippenheim had no hospital and only one doctor, a midwife was enlisted at first. However, it soon became apparent that my mother's pregnancy was problematic, and Dr. Weber was called.

Dr. Weber came to my mother's bedside, at times wearing a Nazi uniform. The nationalistic fever of the early 1930s had touched even Kippenheim. After Adolf Hitler, Germany's new chancellor, came into power on January 30, 1933, life soon changed drastically, especially for the Jewish population in

Germany. Despite his membership in the Nazi Party, Dr. Weber still took good care of his Jewish patients.

Hitler's tirades and hatred against the Jews were beginning to take hold, but many Jewish families, including my parents, did not pay much attention to the new chancellor's growling and insulting speeches against the Jews. Papa dismissed Hitler's words, saying, "I am a disabled veteran of World War I. I was awarded the Iron Cross, and I am a true German patriot." Papa would always bear the scars from shrapnel that had torn into his right shoulder during World War I. He would never again be able to raise his right arm properly, due to his wounds.

Mama and her only sibling, a brother, were born in Jebenhausen — an even smaller village than Kippenheim, about two hundred miles away from us. Mama's father was a cattle dealer. Papa's father was also a cattle dealer, who sold skins and hides. Many Jews in southern Germany practiced this occupation. Papa had four sisters and a deceased brother. His parents had died before his marriage to Mama.

Papa, a textile merchant, had no desire to continue in his father's business. He preferred to work with clean hands rather than to handle the piles of bad-smelling salted cattle hides. The Jews in general owned small shops or were in the cattle business, and many of the Christians of Kippenheim were farmers.

Christians and Jews lived side-by-side and had good relations with each other. Anti-Jewish feelings reared their ugly heads only on rare occasions. Christians went to church on Sunday, while Jews celebrated their Sabbath on Saturday. The different celebrations of the holidays did not bring clashes between the people; rather, they added to the mosaic of village life.

For the most part the Jewish community isolated itself, somewhat by the circumstance of different professions and lifestyles, and somewhat by choice. However, everyone was linked together by his or her shared patriotism and passion for Germany. All Germans fought side-by-side in the wars, defending and dying for their country, Jews and non-Jews alike.

My parents belonged to the middle class. We had a sleep-in maid, and sometimes an extra cleaning lady to take care of our large house. Papa owned a shiny, big black car, which I loved to ride in. He was one of the few in the village who owned such a luxury. Whenever possible Mama helped in the business, especially with the bookkeeping. Papa's territory covered the inns of the Black Forest and the households of neighboring villages. His sheets, pillowcases and towels filled many a future bride's hope chest.

The center of Jewish life was the synagogue. Most of the Jewish people of Kippenheim attended Sabbath services on Saturday mornings and on holidays. It was hard to keep a secret in such a small community. The Jewish population was close-knit, and everyone knew each other's family history, including any skeletons in the closet. There could be no secrets; everything was in the public domain.

Being the youngest member of our congregation was beneficial to me, and I used this to my advantage. I was able to get away with almost anything. For instance, though separation of sexes is mandated in orthodox Jewish worship, many times I left my mother's side in the women's section on the balcony and snuck down to the main sanctuary, where I sat next to my father in the men's quarter.

When I was sitting with the men, Max, a distant cousin, often instigated me to cause problems. He would point to the bright chandeliers hanging over our heads like halos. "See the beautiful lights!" he whispered to me, hoping I would respond. To his joy, I usually repeated his statement loudly. And of course my chatter disrupted the mood and solemnity of the prayers. I was then about three years old, and the parishioners immediately hissed, putting their fingers to their mouths. "Quiet! You must be respectful!"

I felt so ashamed that I cried. Sobbing loudly, I reached for the safety of my father's arms and body, burying myself and trying to disappear. Papa gave Max one of his most threatening looks, and told him to stop his mischief. "Leave the child alone. Don't you have something better to do? Continue your praying!"

There was always a festive spirit during our holidays. Congregants came dressed in their finest clothing. New outfits were bought for special holidays like Rosh Hashanah, the Jewish New Year. I remember my Sabbath dress, maroon velvet with a white collar, sewn especially for me. The outfit was completed with a white hat that covered my thick and curly head of dark brown hair. I felt like a fairy princess when I wore it.

Mama made sure that I was brought up with a good dose of religion. She would sit next to me on my bed every night and listen to me saying my prayers. She taught me the proper Hebrew ones, and I was encouraged to add my own version of wishes and special messages to God, in German.

It was common practice to visit one another after worship, and to invite strangers into our home for dinner. I especially remember the visits of Mr. Nissensohn, a poor Jewish man from Poland. He sold buttons and thread to the Kippenheim populace — mostly to the Jewish people, who bought from him mainly out of pity rather than from necessity. Our meals were probably the only good food he had all week. We usually had chicken noodle soup, followed by short ribs of beef, potato and lettuce salad. Mr. Nissensohn ate with appreciation and great appetite.

In Kippenheim, I had only Jewish friends. My playmates were mostly boys, all older than I, and I was often left alone to play games by myself. But since we had a live-in maid, who performed most of the household chores, Mama was able to spend a great deal of time with me.

My favorite place to play was in our courtyard. Papa had placed some sand in the corner. I filled pails with sand and pretended to bake the most delicious cakes, just like Mama did every Friday for the Sabbath meals. To my dismay, one day a cat found its way to my favorite place and soiled my special play area. I screamed in horror when this happened: "Mama, Mama that bad cat did it again." Mama came to my rescue and removed the mess. Once in a while I could see the culprit's tail, when he or she sneaked out of the courtyard, but I kept as vigilant a watch on my sand as I could.

My doll carriage with my doll Marlene stood nearby. Marlene sat like a princess on her throne, watching my every move. My doll had been a gift from Grandma for my second birthday. She must have felt lonely, since I was not paying much attention to her these days. I was too busy baking my "cakes."

Many years later, as an adult, I discovered that my doll had been produced especially for the 1936 Olympics held in Berlin, which was presided over by Adolf Hitler. "Marlene" had a special hairdo called the "Olympic Roll," and had blue eyes and blond hair to represent the ideal of the Aryan race. The doll factory named the model "Inge," a very popular girl's name at that time. I had no knowledge of this fact at the time when I named my doll after the famous movie star, Marlene Dietrich, who also had blue eyes and blond hair.

My hometown, Kippenheim

Our house in Kippenheim (second from left)

Inge in her sandbox, 1937

Inge in her holiday outfit, 1937

Inge in her Dirndl dress, 1938

Inge in front, grandparents in middle, parents in back
Kippenheim, 1938

Prelude to Disaster

The situation for the Jews changed drastically in 1938. Germany had been defeated and left humiliated in World War I. Depression in spirit and economy enveloped the country. Adolf Hitler seized the opportunity to promise Germany the seemingly impossible: to make it a great power again, and to solve all its problems.

Germany embraced the charismatic Austrian-born failed artist with open arms. His continued spewing of venom against the Jews did not bother most of the people, who willingly accepted the scapegoating as an answer to all their woes.

Large boisterous meetings in beer halls and auditoriums generated much excitement. It was as if Germany were on fire, fanned by the flames of hatred against all enemies of the new National Socialist, or Nazi, Party, but especially against the Jews.

The newly-composed song that contained the lyrics, "When Jewish blood drips from the knife, it tastes twice as good," was sung with great spirit by marchers in the perpetually held parades. New flags bearing the twisted cross, or swastika, flew from many street poles and Gentile homes, and were proudly held high by the enthusiastic paraders as they marched down the streets.

Anti-Jewish voices were becoming louder each day, soon reaching a feverish pitch. Now everyone had to listen to them, to finally take them seriously. The voices were everywhere. Jews watched in horror when their Gentile neighbors gave the Nazi salute, "Heil Hitler!"

In synagogue on the Sabbath, rumors that some Jewish families planned to leave Kippenheim for safer havens were whispered secretly among the congregants. Papa had been hearing the ugly screams and warnings along with everyone else, but he still brushed them off halfheartedly. We lived very close to the borders of France and Switzerland, and Papa commented, "If things get too hot, we can always make a dash for the borders. We still don't have to worry yet!"

His words would soon have little meaning. The turbulent storm was about to strike even the sleepy little village of Kippenheim.

Kristallnacht

My childhood was irreparably disrupted on November 10, 1938. The immense storm clouds that had been threatening Jewish lives finally burst with thundering vengeance. It was a cold November morning, almost two months before my fourth birthday.

Kristallnacht, the "Night of Broken Glass," began on November 9, 1938, in Germany, Austria and part of Czechoslovakia called the Sudetenland. It lasted two horrifying days.

Almost all Jewish houses of worship were severely decimated, and where possible, burned to the ground. Jewish homes and stores were looted and destroyed. Shattered glass lay everywhere in the Jewish houses.

Many Jewish men were arrested and sent to concentration camps. Those who resisted were badly beaten or shot to death.

My grandparents had come to visit us in Kippenheim, and were caught along with us in the unforgettable terror. Grandpa had gone to the synagogue early for the morning prayer. He had no clue that on that day he would be arrested without cause other than that he was Jewish, and that he would be sent to the Dachau concentration camp in Germany.

Not even the synagogue could offer safety to its worshippers. Men wearing the traditional prayer shawls, deep in prayer, felt safe in the embrace of the cloth draped over their shoulders. They thought that the Almighty's arms surrounded them and would shield them from harm. But this time it was different. There was no protection anywhere.

Papa was rudely awakened by a loud banging on the front door. It was the police, come to arrest him. He was told to report to the courtyard of the City Hall, where he would join all the other Jewish men of Kippenheim. Not even the teenage boys above the age of 16 were spared.

Some of the sacred Torah scrolls, which were made of parchment and handwritten, were removed from the sanctuary, torn apart and draped around the fearful men who were gathered together, in total disrespect for their religion.

Only women and children were left behind in the village. Although the synagogue was set afire, the flames were quickly extinguished for fear that the neighboring Christian houses might also suffer damage. Nevertheless, the whole inside of the building had been harmed, and the holy sanctuary was desecrated. The tablet containing the Ten Commandments was dislodged from its perch on top of the structure and thrown to the ground. This served as a warning that from that point on, laws of decency and humanity were dead.

A long night, one that would plunge most of Europe into darkness, was approaching.

I remember standing in the living room with Grandma and Mama, who was holding my hand tightly. Our maid Liesa had recently left us, feeling that it was too dangerous for her to continue employment in a Jewish home.

We clung to each other as stones flew through our windows, shattering them one by one. Pieces of glass fell all around us, covering the floor with the glittering, jagged pieces.

We could hear the sound of breaking glass throughout our large seventeen-room house. One of the hoodlums peered through a broken window, noticing the still-intact chandelier hanging from the ceiling. We heard a bloodcurdling cry coming from the street.

"Quick, let's smash this one!" And a brick hit its mark, barely missing me.

Mama silently pulled me to safety. We ran through the house swiftly, fleeing to a secluded shed in the courtyard of our house. There we stood in complete silence, hardly breathing, cowering in fear. We prayed that the mob would not storm the house and find us.

The thugs kept banging loudly on the large door that gave entrance to our courtyard, which was where Papa parked his large black car. We remained in the shed, clinging to each other in desperation and fear. Fortunately, they did not succeed in breaking down the door and capturing us, though I was sure they could hear the loud hammering of my heart.

Finally the rioting stopped. The silence of the night clothed the earlier fury. We waited, still not moving, hoping that the hoodlums were not tricking us, not secretly waiting to discover us in our hiding place.

More time elapsed, but we could hear no repetition of the screams and loud banging on the door. Mama decided that we should leave the shed. Once again running silently, we reached the home of our Jewish neighbors, where we spent the night. Their windows had also been broken, and the men of their household arrested.

Eventually all the shattered windows were boarded up to keep out the cold November wind. We were made personally responsible for the damage, and had to pay for the replacement windows with our fast dwindling money.

The entire Jewish community was in a state of shock. The hateful words we had been hearing on the radio had come true.

Miraculously, Papa and Grandpa were released from the Dachau concentration camp a few weeks later. They had both been dreadfully mistreated. They spoke of the humiliation of standing in the bitter cold on the parade grounds for hours, wearing nothing but their blue-and-white striped uniforms. If a prisoner so much as blew his nose, he was hosed down with ice-cold water. This happened to my father a few times.

They were all housed together in overcrowded wooden barracks and given small food rations. Even Papa's World War I record and the Iron Cross he'd received for his war injury had no effect on the guards. Papa and Grandpa had a rude awakening of how Jews were to be treated in the "New Order."

Our synagogue in Kippenheim, 1938

The original interior of our synagogue

The interior of our synagogue in 1938, after its destruction

On the Move

Our lives changed drastically when Papa returned from Dachau. We had finally awakened from our slumber of complacency. It was time to leave Germany. But Papa had hesitated too long, and the doors to the free world had almost completely shut.

Early in 1939, we packed most of our personal belongings, sold our house and furniture for a low price, and moved to my grandparents' house in Jebenhausen. We still had hopes of leaving Germany, and therefore planned to stay in Jebenhausen for only a short time.

My grandparents were the last Jewish family living in Jebenhausen, although the population of the small village had been almost half Jewish before the late 1850s. Some of the Jewish families had left for America, and others had moved to a larger neighboring town.

I had often visited my grandparents in Jebenhausen before our move and had many friends there. Some of the happiest memories of my short childhood go back to the two years I spent in Jebenhausen.

I had never thought of myself as being different from my Gentile friends in Jebenhausen. Although anti-Jewish feelings had become even more virulent after the massive November riots, the children and most of the populace of Jebenhausen were not yet infested with the disease of hatred. The children continued their friendships with me, including me in their games as they had before.

It was I who led my friends as we marched up and down the hilly street in front of my grandparents' house, singing the popular songs, which often contained Nazi propaganda. None of us understood the deeper meaning of the songs. Their infectious rhythms enticed us, and everyone was singing them. Why not us?

I remember going into Grandpa's stable, which as was the custom in those days was actually part of the house, beneath our living quarters. There were separate entrances going into the house and into the stable. If I was lucky, Grandpa let me ride one of the docile cows. I helped Grandma chase her chicken flock into their home at night. One of them would become part of our Sabbath meal. Grandma had a small vegetable garden in an alley next to the house. She grew lettuce, parsley and chives. There was not much space to grow more. These gave a good taste to her salads and soups, since the vegetables were freshly picked. Life was uncomplicated and pleasant.

I loved walking barefoot in the meadows with my friends. My grandparents owned land and fruit orchards. It was a great pleasure to bite into the crisp apples that we shook from the trees. Grandma was a wonderful cook and baker. Her pies and cakes always graced our festive Sabbath and holiday table.

I was my grandparents' only grandchild, and I was totally spoiled by them. My parents were quite strict with me, but I could do no wrong in my grandparents' eyes. That of course was another reason that I found life so enjoyable in their home!

Changes

My grandparents' maid, Therese, had been in their employ for twenty-five years, but since Mama could now help with the chores, Therese was no longer needed. Although it was not wise for Therese to continue to work for Jews, she continued her friendship with us, and eventually helped us in many ways.

Papa was forced by the Nazi Order to sell his textile business, and Grandpa sold his last cows. We had to live off our savings, and found our money diminishing rapidly. Our standard of living was suddenly critically changed, since no new money was coming in. We now bought only the necessities needed to sustain our lives.

Grandpa's wish to die in his own home was soon granted. He had never wanted to leave his beloved hometown, Jebenhausen, and his chronically sick heart had weakened even more during his stay in Dachau. He peacefully entered into eternal sleep in May 1939, cradled in my parents' arms. This was a great shock for all of us. I missed Grandpa's friendship and his loving embraces. There was a deep wound left in our hearts.

Life was getting increasingly more difficult for Jews. Jebenhausen was not spared from the anti-Jewish laws. New restrictive decrees were announced every day. Our hope of leaving Germany was now only a memory.

Jews were compelled to give up all their gold and silver. They had to take Israel or Sara as a middle name to make them recognizable as Jews. My name became Inge Sara Auerbacher.

Some of the villagers of Jebenhausen continued their friendship with us, even though Christians were forbidden to associate with Jews. We were no longer permitted to shop in certain stores. A few of the farmers came at night under the cover of darkness to give us some much-needed food. Therese placed food behind my grandfather's gravestone at night for us to pick up in the morning. She was able to save a few of our things until after the war, including two photo albums and some of our prayer books.

By associating with us, the people who helped us risked their lives. They were incredibly brave, and heroes in my eyes.

Every phase of life was changed for the Jews; they were practically not permitted to breathe. The Nazi goal was utter degradation. The children had to attend schools especially set up for Jews. To humiliate the Jews even more, in late 1941 they were forced to sew the yellow Star of David with the word "Jude" in Hebrew-like script on the left side of their clothing, right above the heart. Not even children were spared from this insult.

I needed special "travel permission" documents to attend the only Jewish school, which was located in Stuttgart, in the province of Wuerttemberg in southern Germany. Jews were no longer allowed to travel freely at will without written consent. I had to walk two miles to Goeppingen, a larger neighboring town, and then travel one hour by train, by myself, to attend classes in Stuttgart.

As a six-year-old child, it was dangerous for me to ride alone. The Gentile children around me often taunted and heckled me. "You dirty Jew!" they jeered. Papa told me to sit near the left window and lean against it, in order to unobtrusively cover my yellow badge, even though it was strictly forbidden to hide the so-called "mark of shame."

I remember only one incident of kindness: a Gentile woman left a brown paper bag filled with rolls next to my seat on the train. She must have felt sorry for the little Jewish child traveling by herself. This stranger was also a hero to me, since any association with Jews could result in severe punishment — even in death.

One morning I noticed a group of poorly-clothed men on the train, guarded by a German soldier. They must have been foreign slave laborers. I was curious and tried to listen to their conversations. It was not German, and I therefore understood nothing.

The guard opened a can of food and gave it to one of the men. He took a spoon and ate quickly from it. The can made the round to the other prisoners. Each man took his spoon to get his share. The prisoners looked very thin and seemed very hungry. I felt sorry for them and wondered where they were being taken to, and what kind of work they would have to perform. I had seen such prisoners in Goeppingen before, and my parents told me they came from Poland. I had no idea where that country was, and found their language strange. It had absolutely no similarity to German.

The yellow Star of David, emblazoned with the word *Jude* (Jew)

1941

None of our family living in foreign countries was able to help us leave Germany. All their efforts failed: we had waited too long to judge the danger and act upon it. Our fate was sealed. Escape was no longer possible.

The "Final Solution," the Nazi plan for the total liquidation of all Jews in Europe, began in 1941, when the first deportations to "the East" began.

One day in early December of 1941, my grandmother, my parents and I received our order for transport. Papa was afraid of the unknown destination. Could this resettlement in "the East" be to a place like Dachau?

Papa and Mama composed a letter to the Gestapo (the secret police), pleading with them to spare us because of Papa's World War I injuries acquired fighting for Germany. Papa's request succeeded for us, but we were not able to help my grandmother.

I shall never forget our tearful good-byes, watching Grandma descend the stairs in the Stuttgart Railroad Station. I wanted time to slow down, to be able to hold onto her image as long as possible. But suddenly the stairs were empty.

I remained standing as if frozen in time. We did not know it then that Grandma and many of my classmates were being deported to Riga in Latvia. The "Nazi Mobile Killing Forces" shot almost all of them in a nearby forest shortly after their arrival in Riga.

I remember that after Grandma was taken away, I cried myself to sleep every night. I covered my head with the warm down comforter, hoping that it would block the sound of my sobs so that my parents would not hear me. Every night I prayed for my beloved grandmother's safe return, but my prayers were never answered.

Soon after my grandmother's deportation, we were forced out of my grandparents' home, receiving no monetary compensation. The German State owned my grandparents' house now.

We were relocated to one of the "Jewish" houses in the neighboring town of Goeppingen. My parents were forced to work for very little money in a women's undergarment factory. The Jewish school in Stuttgart closed before I completed my first grade.

The air raid sirens awakened us many nights. I was petrified to hear their screaming sound. Sometimes I saw a red horizon in the distance, caused by the fires of the Allied bombs being dropped on their targets. We did not always go down to the basement, which served as an air raid shelter.

Deportation

Deportation to "the East" became more frequent during the following months. None of us knew that "the East" meant a death sentence. But we had fears and doubts about the designation. We knew that it meant something bad for the Jews.

Our turn came on August 22, 1942, when we received our orders for transport. I was now number "XIII-1-408" — the youngest in our transport of about 1200 people. I was only seven years old, a person without any citizenship.

There was no longer any way to avoid being sent away. The directive contained many instructions, which had to be faithfully followed. All our money was taken from us, and we were told what belongings we could take along: no knives or other sharp implements were allowed, but metal dishes and spoons were permissible.

The police came to our apartment and Mama was ordered to place the house keys on the dining room table. The official then said in a demeaning tone of voice, "Now you can go!"

We were forced to enter a school gymnasium in Goeppingen, where we were searched, along with all our belongings. I was terribly afraid that my doll, Marlene, would be taken from me. Since Grandma's deportation, Marlene was the only token of remembrance I had of her, and I was intent on holding onto her for dear life. To my dismay and horror, an official tore Marlene violently from my arms. He did not listen to my cry of desperation, but pulled at the rubber bands holding her head and appendages.

He looked inside her hollow body to see if any valuables were hidden. I watched him in horror, tears streaming down my face. Would he destroy my beloved Marlene?

After a few minutes, he seemed satisfied with his search and gave back my precious doll. I made a vow never to let Marlene be mistreated by anyone else again. But my luck ran out when the same official took a liking to the wooden Dutch boy pin I was wearing. He tore it off my dress, saying, "You won't need this where you are going!" He probably had another little girl to give it to — a daughter, niece or cousin.

From Goeppingen we were taken to Stuttgart, which was the main gathering place for Jews who were being deported. We were brought to a large building in a park called Killesberg, used previously for flower shows. Jews from all over the province of Wuerttemberg were housed in two huge halls. There were many old people and decorated war veterans among them.

We bedded down on the bare floor, using our duffle bags as pillows. There were only a few chairs for the entire group of over 1000 people. We received some food from the community kitchen. We were all in a state of shock. "Where are they taking us, what will happen to us there?" Rumors abounded that we were being sent to a ghetto where the able-bodied would work, and we would be given comfortable living quarters. Some people lost their minds, and their screams were heard throughout the long night.

After two days, trucks took us to a train waiting at the Stuttgart Railroad Station. It was a passenger train, and we were cramped into the cars like sardines in a can. The doors were locked and storm troopers guarded our every move. We had some food with us, but water was very scarce. I remember having an upset stomach, which happened to me whenever I was nervous. I became a great challenge to the other passengers as the stench of vomit filled the car.

We traveled further into the East. The landscape changed and I saw signs with words I could not understand. They were no longer in the German language.

After two days the train stopped in a town called Bohusovice, in Czechoslovakia. We were told to disembark, to leave everything behind except a rolled-up blanket, knapsack and metal dishes. The storm troopers screamed, "March, don't lag behind!" They had guns and used whips to keep us in line.

I held my doll and dragged a small knapsack on the ground. My parents placed me between them to protect me from the whiplashes. Many old people were lying on the side of the road; they were not able to keep up the tempo of the march. Close to two miles later a walled town appeared. It soon swallowed us up. We were brought to an underground cell for a body and belongings search.

The collection center for deportation in Stuttgart

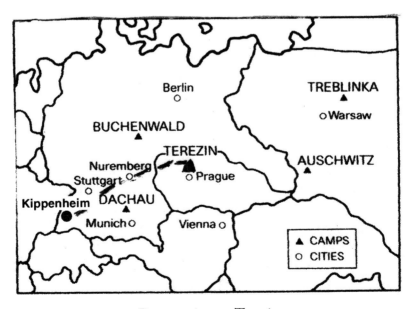

Deportation to Terezin

Terezin Concentration Camp

We had arrived at the Terezin concentration camp in Czechoslovakia, *Theresienstadt* as it was called in German. Terezin had large brick barracks, underground cells and old broken-down houses in very poor condition. It was isolated from the outside world by high walls, deep water-filled trenches, wooden fences and barbed wire. Communication with the outside world was strictly forbidden.

Terezin was located about forty miles north of Prague. Hapsburg Emperor Joseph II built it in 1780 in memory of his mother, Empress Maria Theresa. It was initially a garrison town, abandoned by the military in the 1880s and then settled by a few thousand civilians.

By the end of 1941, Terezin had been emptied and readied by high-ranking Nazi officials to serve as a transit camp for Jewish deportees. From Terezin, the prisoners were slated for extermination in the gas chambers of Auschwitz and other death camps located mostly in Nazi-occupied Poland.

All our clothing except what we wore was confiscated upon our arrival. We never saw our suitcases again. I arrived in Terezin thankfully still holding my doll in my arms, dragging a small knapsack, a metal dish and spoon.

The inmates of Terezin were mostly from Czechoslovakia, some from other countries in Europe. They came from all walks of life and from different professions. Some of them were of mixed

Jewish and Christian origins; being only part-Jewish was sufficient credential to earn you a place in a concentration camp.

Terezin was a gruesome place. Our first living quarters were in the attic of a large brick army barracks. We slept on the bare floor using our blanket and knapsack as a cushion. Hundreds of people moved hopelessly in this dark, hot area, often stumbling over the covered bodies of the dead. Some people lost their will to live and jumped from the small attic openings to their deaths in the courtyard.

These terrible conditions brought out the best and worst behavior in people. Mrs. Rinder, a Czech woman, found me lying in misery on the floor one day. She, her husband and young son had arrived earlier from Prague. This good woman, a total stranger, gave me part of her son's mattress and brought me to a children's room in the same building.

The room was very crowded. Some children slept on double-deck bunk beds, and many like me on small mattresses on the floor. I could not speak with most of the children, since they spoke Czech. There were only a few German-speaking children in the room. Some of the children appeared to be sick with a fever and stayed in their beds all day. It was whispered that the children had scarlet fever. I was depressed and homesick for my parents who were still living in the hot attic.

After a short time, I also contracted scarlet fever, and spent four months in the so-called hospital. I was in a room whose peeling walls were covered with flies. Two children occupied each bed. Measles, mumps and a double middle-ear infection followed. I was infested with worms, lost my voice, and my body was covered with boils. I was not expected to live.

My parents were not allowed to visit me for the entire duration of my stay in the hospital, but miraculously, just before my eighth birthday, I recovered. Before leaving the hospital I was washed in a large bucket containing a disinfecting solution. My hair had been cut very short to help rid me of lice. I was ready to be united with my parents. Nothing else mattered.

Most men, women and children were housed in separate quarters. I was fortunate to be allowed to stay with my parents in the disabled war veterans' section.

Life was harsh and strange and without any privacy. We slept on the floor, or when fortunate on straw-filled mattresses on overcrowded double and triple-deck bunk beds. The living quarters were unbearably hot in the summer and very cold in winter. We shared a tiny room with a family from Berlin two out of the three years we spent at Terezin.

The family had a daughter, Ruth, who was two months older than I. Her father walked with a limp caused by a World War I injury. Ruth and I became best friends. She and her parents slept on the lower bunk, we on the upper. Ruth's father was half-Christian and half-Jewish, and although her mother was Jewish, Ruth had been raised as a devout Christian. This made no difference in terms of their incarceration.

I made a bed for my doll in a carton near my head. One day I found a dead mouse in the box. Not even a little mouse could find enough food to survive in this hell.

We stood in line three times a day, our metal dishes in hand, to receive our daily food rations from the community kitchens. Bread, potatoes and soup were the most important words in our vocabulary. Breakfast consisted of "coffee," a dark-colored liquid that had a terrible taste. Lunch was a watery soup, a potato, and a small portion of turnips or a sauce containing slivers of horsemeat. Dinner was mainly soup. I remember Mama marking off each day on our rationed bread supply to make sure that we would have enough left to last the week.

Whenever a new transport arrived, we questioned the people, asking if they had been able to smuggle in any onions or garlic. My father usually approached the newcomers. If he was lucky, someone would part with a small onion or a few cloves of garlic. We cut the precious morsels into small pieces and placed them on a piece of bread. I remember the wonderful taste it left in my mouth. I held onto the aroma for a long time without rinsing my mouth, savoring the rare taste. Onions especially were as valuable as pearls to us.

There were constant epidemics, due to overcrowding and lack of hygiene. We pumped most of our water from polluted wells. It was very hard to keep clean, since we were permitted very few showers in the community bathhouse — men in one room at one time, women and children together in the same room another time. Rats, mice, fleas and bedbugs were a constant menace to us. I can still feel the awful stomach cramps from dysentery, which afflicted everyone, and the long walks to the latrines, which were crowded and without privacy.

One of my friends had another sickness. We were told to stay away from her, that her illness was very bad and very contagious. It was called tuberculosis. However, when I noticed that she was receiving small portions of extra food and a little milk, I wanted the same, and prayed that I too would get this illness, and the extra food that went along with it.

Soon I had the same symptoms. I was tired all the time, lost a lot of weight and coughed a lot. When I was tested for tuberculosis, the result was positive. I, too, had tuberculosis. My prayers had been answered. Little did I know how sick this illness would make me, and the consequences that would arise from it, both in the concentration camp and in my later life. Although I, too, got some extra rations, no other treatment was available.

Almost all the adults were forced to work. Some women spliced mica, a product needed for the war effort. Mama's first job was washing laundry from typhus patients. Although she had no training in nursing, she later worked as a nurse in the old people's section for sick women. Every day Papa rummaged in the garbage dump in search of potato peelings and rotten turnips, cutting edible parts from them to supplement our meager diet. We lived in constant fear that we would be sent further East into the unknown, where conditions might be even worse than in Terezin.

I was part of a group of children who lived in our compound. Our bodies became thinner with each passing day, and our bones began to show through our skin. Still, we continued to play, scouring in the garbage heaps hoping to find a treasure — a rotten turnip, potato peelings or a piece of string. School was absolutely forbidden, but some heroic teachers taught us in so-called "keeping busy classes," mostly from memory since there were very few books or school supplies.

The most frightening day of my three years at Terezin was the Bohusovice Ravine roll call on November 11, 1943. We were told that some inmates were missing, and a complete count of us had to be taken.

At least 40,000 of us were herded onto a large muddy field. It was a cold, rainy day, and our feet sank into the ground. We were surrounded by soldiers pointing their guns at us. Our future was uncertain.

No food was given to us all day, and no toilets were available. Brutal storm troopers counted and beat many people. This was the only time during my incarceration that I was outside the camp, but the frightening and dangerous circumstances did not permit me to appreciate it.

Late at night we were ordered to return to Terezin. Men, women and children were told to walk back separately. My parents and I refused to be apart, and held onto each other tightly as we walked. I watched in horror as one of the storm troopers smashed the butt of his rifle into my mother's back for defying orders. Many dead people were left on the field, but we somehow made it back without further punishment.

Rumors of mass murder in the East had begun to circulate by the end of 1943. The International Red Cross finally requested a visit to a camp, and Terezin was chosen for the inspection.

Just before the visit in June 1944, Terezin went through a "beautification" program. Houses were painted, street signs replaced numbered blocks. Markers to school and playgrounds were put up. A band shell was erected with musicians playing, pretending that Terezin was a spa for Jews to live in. Some children were given sardine sandwiches, and a children's opera was performed for the visitors. New worthless camp money was issued. Only healthy people were allowed to walk in the restricted area shown to the group.

The commission believed the deception and wrote a glowing report about the camp and the wonderful conditions in which the Jews were being given the opportunity to live.

Terezin was the antechamber to Auschwitz. Transports reached a crescendo during the Jewish High Holidays in the fall of 1944. Adolf Eichmann, who was in charge of the transportation of all Jews in Europe to the killing centers, visited Terezin many times. I remember seeing him and his black car.

When the last selections to the East were about to be made, all remaining war veterans were ordered to appear at SS headquarters. A red circle was drawn around my family's names. We had been spared from certain death.

But my best friend Ruth, her parents, and most of my other friends had not fared so well. They were herded into the waiting cattle cars; the doors were bolted and their fate was sealed. Within a few days of their departure, their lives were snuffed out in the gas chambers of Auschwitz.

I was lonely and missed Ruth and my other playmates. At the time I didn't know what had happened to them.

One day soon after Ruth and the others were taken away, a young woman stopped me as I stood near where I lived with my parents. She seemed nervous and in distress. Speaking quickly, she asked, "Can you help me take care of my little boy, Benny? I work in the kitchen and they changed my schedule to day work. I'll reward you with a few potatoes."

I looked at the toddler sitting in a makeshift stroller. He was smiling at me. I was nine years old, and proud to bring the precious payment of a few potatoes to my parents. I accepted the terms of employment and carefully looked after my new little charge while his mother worked.

Meanwhile, orders were given to build gas chambers at Terezin, but they were never completed. Terezin was almost empty by early 1945. As the Allies approached, prisoners still under Nazi rule were forced on death marches, with orders to relocate many of them to our under-populated camp.

The prisoners were in horrible shape. Some were forced to walk long distances. Their feet were wrapped in rags, or they wore shabby wooden sandals. Their heads were shaved and they were dressed in blue-and-white striped prison uniforms or torn clothing. There were more men than women in the groups.

At times the "luckier" ones traveled part of the distance in open or sometimes completely closed freight trains. They all looked like walking skeletons, and many suffered from typhus and other diseases. Most of them had been traveling for some time, and they all appeared very dirty, almost inhuman.

We shared some of our meager food rations with these unfortunate people. They fought like hungry animals over the morsels of bread that we threw to them.

When news spread that the people from Riga were coming, I searched in vain for my grandmother. We had heard rumors back home that Grandma's transport had been sent to Riga, in Latvia. To our dismay and shock, though, we now heard the horrible truth of the shootings in the forests, and the gassings in Auschwitz. These horrific happenings had been kept secret from us at Terezin.

The war was not yet over. Fear spread throughout the camp. "Now they will also kill us!" we all thought.

The population of Terezin reached a few thousand more with the influx of the newcomers. Most of the new arrivals were young and were barely out of their teens, but despite their youth the death rate of the newcomers was very high. Our stretched population cowered at what new horrors might lie ahead of us.

Terezin

Standing on line for food at Terezin

Liberation

The war was coming to an end in the beginning of May 1945. I saw partially burned pieces of paper floating through the air; the guards were busy destroying the evidence of death and destruction. I remember hearing a lot of noise as the fleeing guards drove away in their trucks. I climbed a wooden fence to see what was happening. A hand grenade thrown by one of the guards landed very close to me and I ran to my parents for safety.

My father's military experience came in handy. He immediately found a dark abandoned cellar, and we quickly followed him there. I left Marlene on the bed, taking only a small prayer book that my father had found in a pile of garbage. Someone before leaving on the death train must have lost faith in God, even after smuggling it into the camp, or was afraid to take it on the journey. His name inside the book was still visible.

More people joined us in the cellar. One person had a small candle that brought a little light into the darkness. I prayed with all my heart and read from the prayer book, the "Shema," the great faith statement of Judaism: "Hear O Israel, the Lord our God, the Lord is One." My lips trembled as I cried out to God to save us.

A brave man decided to leave the cellar to see what was going on. He returned quickly, out of breath and shouting, "We are free, the Russians are here!"

There was doubt in our hearts. Could it be true that this nightmare was finally over? We walked carefully up the dark steps from the dungeon that served as our hiding place. There was much commotion on the street; trucks and tanks emblazoned with the Red Star were everywhere. The soldiers were dancing and singing with joy on top of the tanks. Some even played the accordion. It was a strange sight.

The night of May 8, 1945 will forever remain in my thoughts. Liberation had finally come, and this date became my second birthday, which I would celebrate equally as my actual day of birth.

I was ten years old and I felt that I had already lived a lifetime. My first act in my newfound freedom was to tear off the yellow Star of David from my clothing. We returned to our living quarters late at night, but we remained dressed in our clothes still with many doubts in our thoughts. "Are we really free? What will happen next?"

The Soviet army was ill-equipped and had limited food supplies. Despite this, the soldiers shared some of their rations with us. We received generous portions of barley soup. I remember a kind Russian soldier handing me a piece of black bread, with what seemed like a mountain of butter.

Only a few thousand survivors were left alive in Terezin. From 1941 to 1945, a total of 140,000 Jewish people were sent to Terezin, of whom 88,000 were shipped to the killing centers of the East, while another 35,000 died of malnutrition or disease. Out of the 15,000 children sent to Terezin, very few survived. I was lucky to be one of them. The camp remained on quarantine for some months after our liberation because of a typhus epidemic. We were free at last, and yet not fully free.

Homeward Bound

In early July 1945, a bus from the city of Stuttgart finally picked us up. It felt as if a carriage had descended from heaven to take us away from the man-made hell of Terezin. There were 13 survivors from our original transport of about 1200 people. Among them were my parents and I. It was a miracle that a complete family had managed to survive the Nazi death machine. I remember riding through bombed-out cities where only the foundations of houses were visible — one of them was the formerly beautiful city of Dresden.

During my trip, I could feel something burning and itching on my leg. This would be the last flea to bite me, I promised myself as I tried not to scratch.

After a few days on the bus, we were brought to a displaced persons' camp in Stuttgart, a temporary facility that had been prepared to house returning Jewish survivors. I remember my first meal, served on a beautifully set table with a white tablecloth. The meal began with noodle soup. I ate slowly, relishing each spoonful. This was my first good meal in three long years.

After a short stay at this facility, we made our way back to Jebenhausen, where we hoped to be reunited with my grandmother. It soon became apparent, though, that thirteen immediate members of our family would never return home, including my precious Grandma. All of them had lost their lives at the hands of the Nazis, either by starvation, gassing or firing squads. Even our beloved maid Therese became a victim of the war. An American soldier shot through the front door of her house when she did not open the door to satisfy his demand, killing her instantly. She had no knowledge of the English language, and had stood frozen with fear behind the door, not knowing what to do. This was a great shock for all of us.

Our stay in my grandparents' house in Jebenhausen was short. The memories were too painful for us to remain, and we moved into a nicely furnished apartment in Goeppingen. Papa resumed his textile business, and eventually owned a car once again.

Very few Jewish children had survived in the province of Wuerttemberg or elsewhere in Europe. I had lost almost four years of school, and was placed in the fourth and fifth grade classes. It was hard to believe that one could have a normal life after such horror and misery. I had many new friends — all Christian, who treated me well.

Immigration to America

Despite our decent new life, my parents decided to leave Germany less than a year after our return from Terezin. They thought there was no future for me in the blood-drenched land of our birth, even though a "new wind" was blowing in Germany.

As a gesture of good will, President Harry S. Truman opened the doors of America to the Jewish survivors of Hitler's hell. My parents wanted to take advantage of this offer, and they applied to be included on the first list in 1946.

It was now the spring of 1946, and I was eleven years old. Since very few passenger trains were available after the war, cattle cars were used to transport us. None of us minded sleeping on the floor; we were used to such conditions. The nights were cool, and it was chilly in the boxcar. Since I was the youngest in our car, I was given a bed; there were a few cots, but not enough for everyone.

After some days on the train, we arrived in Bremen, and were housed for a short time in a former German army facility. We were then brought to the port of Bremerhaven where the Marine Perch, an American troop transport ship, awaited us.

It was a stormy ten-day crossing. I was seasick, as were many of the passengers for most of the journey. We finally arrived in the New York City Harbor on May 24, 1946. My first view of America was the Statue of Liberty the night before. Her beacon of light reached out to us with a special brightness of welcome.

I walked down the gangplank with my parents, holding Marlene tightly in my arms. We were brought to a large hall where my Aunt Trudl waited for us. Mama had a brother and his wife living in the New York City area, who had managed to leave Germany just before all hell had broken loose in the early 1930s. My uncle was drafted and fought in the American army in World War II.

The Joint Distribution Committee, a charitable Jewish agency, took up sponsorship for the survivors of our group. My aunt and uncle had no funds to help us — they had only their love and some knowledge of how to live in America.

When my parents and I left the arrival area, we walked from the darkness of the past into the sunlight. America embraced us with open arms, with the possibility of hope and a better future.

Consequences of the Holocaust

Unfortunately, our starry eyes of a land of unlimited possibilities soon dimmed. Our hopes and dreams evaporated soon after our arrival in New York City.

We stayed for a while in a small second-floor apartment, which we shared with my mother's brother, his wife and her father. It was located in Rockville Center, a suburb of New York City. My uncle had recently returned home after serving in the American army.

After a short stay with my our Rockville Center family, I was sent to live with distant cousins in Jamaica, Queens, so that I could go to school with their children. Although I had come to this country speaking only a few words of English, I was determined to learn the language quickly, and practiced new words every day.

Within a short time, my parents found jobs as domestics for a wealthy family living on a large estate in Rye, New York. Once again, we moved. We were finally together on our own as a family again.

We had been in America for less than three months when another tragedy struck. I was suffering from what we thought was a bad cold, which was soon diagnosed as a recurring case of the tuberculosis that I had contracted in the concentration camp. I couldn't run anymore; I suffered from constant extreme exhaustion. A severe cough that had been minor for a long time — which my mother attributed to the chilly boxcar we'd stayed in during our train ride to the boat taking us to America— returned with a vengeance. I went from being a healthy child to being a very ill one in what seemed to be no time at all.

We went to see a doctor, who sternly recommended that I see the Chief of Chest Diseases at a hospital in the New York suburbs. In short order our worst fears were confirmed: once again I had pulmonary tuberculosis, which we thought had been cured. The doctor told us that I would have to be confined to a hospital with other sick children.

"No, no, I'm not going to a hospital," I cried, tears streaming down my face. "Don't make me go," I begged my parents. I didn't want to be separated from them again, this time in a strange new country where I hardly knew anyone other than my family. I also knew what a hospital was like from the time at Terezin when I had scarlet fever.

Still crying, I remembered that I had prayed to get this disease while I was in the concentration camp. *Didn't I wish for this so that I would be able to have more food rations?* But then I had felt well again, and I thought that the disease would leave me forever once we were set free. It belonged in the concentration camp, not in the United States, land of the free where everyone had enough food to eat and didn't have to be sick the way I had been.

Didn't I deserve to be happy? What had I done that made me so bad that I got sick again? Didn't God care about me anymore? Please, God, you listened to me before, please, please listen to me again. Don't make me sick in America!

But God didn't listen to me this time. I was taken to Ward 200 at Sunshine Cottage, the children's communicable disease hospital which was part of Grasslands Hospital (now called Westchester Medical Center) in Valhalla, New York. Here in the tuberculosis section of the hospital, I was required to remain on complete bed rest, along with similarly ill children.

There were no magic drugs available at the time. If bed rest didn't work, the only other answer was "pneumothorax," which meant having air pumped into the pleural cavity to collapse the sick lung in order to give it absolute rest. Even with this procedure, the outlook was not a good one, and the disease ultimately consumed many patients. Since this procedure was no guarantee of cure, my parents listened to my wishes and refused to have it done.

However, there were other painful tests. Every other week we had a "gastric" test performed on us. This test consisted of having a long rubber hose (which looked like a snake ready to attack) inserted and guided through the nose and down toward the stomach. It was quite painful, in spite of the piece of ice they gave us to suck on when gagging overwhelmed us. When the proper depth was reached, a syringe was attached to the tube and a liquid was withdrawn, which was sent for analysis to show whether the disease was still active.

The bronchoscopy was an even greater torture. It was performed in the operating room, and the memory of the terrible pain is still strong in my mind. Very little anesthesia was given, and the bad tasting solution, which lightly iced my throat, did not last the length of the procedure. The pain was excruciating, and you couldn't even scream, because the instrument was touching your vocal chords.

Fortunately my parents listened to my pleas not to sign for such a test again, but I truly thought that I was choking to death during the procedure, and was surprised to find that I was actually still alive after it was completed.

Ever so often we were sent to a conference attended by other physicians and resident doctors in training. When it was my turn, I heard the doctor telling the assembly that I had a very bad case, with both of the lungs involved. I was considered one of the sickest children in Ward 200, and was not permitted to leave my bed for almost a year. I had escaped one prison only to be put into another. *Would I ever be able to enjoy freedom again?*

My parents were permitted to visit me once a week for only a few hours. I lived for Sundays when I could see them. Some parents of the other children had gotten tuberculosis and died, leaving their children bereft and alone. I was grateful to have my loving parents.

I was the only Jewish child in the hospital and had no one to share a religious bond. Sometimes I would join the other children when they celebrated their Christian holidays, but I was not able to celebrate my special days, and there was never any provision for me to honor Jewish dietary laws. I had only my doll, Marlene to keep me company, as she had ever since I was two years old — and a radio that my parents gave to me during one of their visits.

I was thirteen years old in 1948, and had spent two years in the hospital. My parents finally convinced the doctors to let me come home, provided that I follow strict orders to rest, not go to school or in any other way to overexert myself. We all celebrated when I was finally not contagious, and I tried to resume a normal life.

Part of my new life was to help my mother earn a little extra money by selling aprons to people in the neighborhood. We climbed up and down steps and worked hard. Although I became tired, I never told my mother, and when I started to spit up blood, I tried to hide the horrific evidence of the blood until it no longer became possible.

This time the doctor from the hospital recommended someone nearer to where we lived, since I was by now too weak to make more than a short trip. The new doctor prescribed an experimental new drug, streptomycin. Miraculously, this worked wonders, and it soon became widely used to cure tuberculosis.

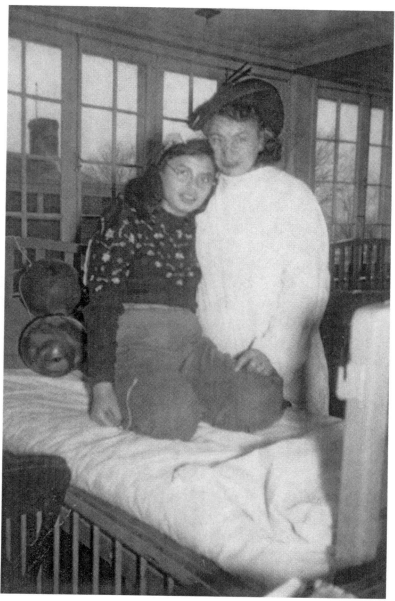

Inge and Mother at the infectious disease hospital, 1947

Aftermath

During my two years in the hospital, my parents rented an apartment in Brooklyn. When I was permitted to join them in 1948, I received home instruction and was able to enter Bushwick High School in 1950, at the age of 15.

This was my first chance to really go to school. I completed high school with honors, in three years instead of the customary four, by attending summer school. My education was interrupted once again in college because of a recurrence of tuberculosis, but again streptomycin, bed rest for a year and a combination of other newly discovered drugs finally cured me.

I graduated from Queens College, part of the City University of New York, with a Bachelor of Science degree in chemistry in 1958. There still was a great stigma attached to tuberculosis, as I discovered on two occasions when I was seriously involved with two young professionals, both of whom rejected me after I was honest enough to tell them about my health history.

I worked for thirty-eight years as a chemist in medical research and diagnostic work.

I am the author of five books on various themes, including the Holocaust, which have been published in many languages. Several documentaries have been made about my life.

I have made it my passion and mission to lecture in many countries to children and adults, in the hope of fostering good will among mankind. Because I never married, I consider the children of the world as "my" children. My motto is: Never Give Up!

Who Am I?

Out of the ashes I was born,
From my family I was torn.
I'm a new link in a broken chain,
I'm all the joy and all the pain.

I'm hope, happiness and sorrow,
I'm yesterday and tomorrow.
I bear the names of unknown faces,
From distant lands and foreign places.

I'm the song that was never heard,
I'm the spirit taking wing like a bird.
I'm the life that our loved ones knew.
I'm their dream that has come true.

I'm so many silent girls and boys,
I was born to live and be their voice.
I'm a tree that will continue to grow,
With branches of those whom I'll never know.

Who am I?

I am, I am!

Inge Auerbacher

About the Authors

Bożenna on left, Inge on right

Inge Auerbacher was born in 1934 in Kippenheim, Germany. She was imprisoned from 1942 to 1945 in the Terezin concentration camp in Czechoslovakia. She immigrated to the United States in 1946, and currently lives in New York City.

Auerbacher graduated from Queens College in New York City with a Bachelor of Science degree in chemistry. She worked for thirty-eight years in medical research and clinical work. She is retired and travels to many countries to speak about the Holocaust and about tolerance.

Author of:

I Am A Star— Child of the Holocaust
Beyond the Yellow Star to America
Running Against the Wind
Finding Dr. Schatz — The Discovery of Streptomycin and A Life It Saved
Highway to New York

Honors and Awards:

- New York State Senate Woman of Distinction, 2009
- Among the first honorees into the New York City Hall of Fame, 2007
- Honorary Doctorate of Humane Letters from Long Island University, New York City, 2005
- Ellis Island Medal of Honor, 1999
- Louis E. Yavner Citizen Award, 1999
- Queens College of the City of New York Alumni Star, 1998
- Many other citations of honor from various governmental agencies

Bożenna Urbanowicz was born in 1934 in Leonowka, a small town in the far eastern province of Wolyn, Poland. In the 1940s, she — along with her parents, brother and two sisters — were transported first to Freiberg, Germany, and then to the Chemnitz Labor Camp, where they remained for the duration of the war.

After the war ended, her family, with the exception of her mother, joined relatives in America. They did not see their mother until several years later, when she found them and came to America.

Urbanowicz studied draping, fashion design and sewing in high school and earned her living in the fashion industry. She is married to Richard V. Gilbride and has four children and three grandsons. She spends much of her time traveling in America and abroad, telling her story of surviving the Holocaust of World War II.

Honors and Awards:
- Commission member of the Founding of the Nassau County Holocaust Learning Center
- Recipient of the Louis E. Yavner Award by the New York State Board of Regents, Department for "Outstanding Contribution to Teaching the Holocaust and other Violations of Human Rights"
- Ellis Island Medal of Honor
- Member of the U.S. Holocaust Memorial Museum, Washington, D.C., where she donated artifacts and gave testimony as a Polish Catholic Holocaust survivor
- Raised funds for the Zegota Monument in Warsaw, Poland
- Awarded "Honorary Righteous Gentile" Medal by the Polish president of Righteous Among Nations, Jerzy P. Sliwczynski
- Received three "Cross of Merit" medals from three Polish presidents

- Associate producer of the documentary *Zegota, Council of Aid to Jews in Occupied Poland 1942-1945*
- Served on the National Polish American-Jewish American Council
- Contributed her story to Professor Richard C. Lukas' book, *Forgotten Survivors*
- Board member, Catholic League for Religious and Civil Rights, Long Island Chapter
- Thirteen other awards, commendations and certificate of merit from senators, congressmen and local civic leaders